this little light

SAKITA L. GILLIAM

Acknowledgments

First and foremost, I would like to thank the Almighty God for giving me the strength to persevere through all of my life challenges, and for not only walking with me, but carrying me through the times I couldn't walk on my own. Thank God for my son, Malachi Reams, who loves me unconditionally, and goes through ups and downs with me. I thank God for my parents, Beverly Gilliam-Singleton and Harry Singleton for supporting me throughout life's journey.

Thank God for my father, Lyndon Taylor, for doing the best he knew how to do. Thank God for my grandparents, Fannie and Robert Gilliam, for being the backbone of my support system.

I would also like to thank my entire family for their support even when they didn't know the intricate parts they played in pushing me toward my God-given purpose.

My heart is so appreciative of Silver Cloud Missionary Baptist Church and the late great Emeritus Pastor Otha V. McDade, who spiritually poured into me my entire childhood.

I'd also like to give honor to my current ministry, Advocate United Church of Christ, and my pastor, Rev. Malcolm Griffith, for cultivating my gift.

Finally, I have to praise God for my mentor, Dr. Easter Watson, for being a great inspiration and for always being a listening ear when I needed one.

"Let your light so shine before men, that they may see your good works, and glorify your Father which is in heaven."
-*Matthew 5:16*

Foreword

The Word of God and our relationship with God is our anchor. The Holy Spirit is able to guide your thoughts and get you to look inwardly about your decisions. The Holy Spirit also puts people and situations in place so that we can learn from them.

"We can rejoice, too, when we run into problems and trials, for we know that they help us develop endurance. And endurance develops strength of character, and character strengthens our confident hope of salvation. And this hope will not lead to disappointment. For we know how dearly God loves us, because he has given us the Holy Spirit to fill our hearts with his love." - Romans 5:3-5 (NLT)

Everything I have gone through in life reminds me of this scripture. In my own spiritual journey I have learned that the journey is never over, but in actuality it is just beginning as we draw closer to God.

I thank God for you inviting me along for the ride by allowing me to share my story with you. Just as God has moved in my life, He will work in yours too. You haven't seen nothing yet! Watch what God does for you and your family. In Jesus' name, Amen.

Rev. Malcolm Griffith
Senior Pastor, Advocate United Church of Christ

Life can be pretty complex. Things can happen that may lead one to feeling worthless and insignificant. This does not mean life hasn't produced any good experiences, but rather that the bad things were so heavy that they seemed to outweigh the good. As time moves forward, life continues to throw challenges that feel as if they are an attempt to ultimately destroy life itself. *But then something shifts.* That thing that once felt like a fire continuously burning within your soul turns into a light that reflects life's purpose. In the pages to follow you will find a story about my life and the light that has not only left permanent marks, but also serves as a guiding light with purpose.

When I think about my life and everything that has come my way, I can do nothing but praise God and thank Him for the revelations that have surfaced from every experience. I've come to realize that every intricate part of my life had a bigger purpose than what I thought as I was going through it.

There were times I felt so low I considered taking matters into my own hands by ending my life. I figured my life didn't matter, because if it did, the things I was suffering through wouldn't be happening to me.

Not only did I struggle to understand why I had to suffer so many challenges, but I was also tackling life in general. I self-sabotaged with thoughts of pain, chaos, and challenges by turning those things into insecurities, doubt, and low self-esteem. My life consisted of internalizing everything that happened to me into a bubble that screamed bondage. Even though this bondage affected many areas of my life, it all stemmed from one source. Some might think that source was other people's actions towards me, but I later found out that my actions and the way I felt had nothing to do with other people. Instead, it surprisingly had everything to do with the way I thought. I struggled with this concept for a while until I realized that my actions followed suit with what I thought and believed.

"For as a man thinketh in his heart, so is he."
Proverbs 23:7

I felt worthless. My thoughts had me going down Victim Avenue. On this avenue, everyone's negative actions towards me either made me feel less than human or less than as a woman.

What a person thinks of themselves is typically reflected in their daily actions.

I have always been a bit reserved and to myself. Most of the time I didn't care what was going on around me. I followed the beat of my own drum. However, there were other times I'd try to fit in with the crowd, only to end up in situations that caused extended periods of darkness.

It seems just like yesterday I was placing blame for my shortcomings and insecurities on the heads of ex-boyfriends, bad men, and my father. Yes, I formulated negative thoughts of myself through a skewed vision of shattered relationships. Because of this, my actions towards people were often based on formulated thoughts from past situations portrayed through poor decisions. In other words, I was exhibiting behaviors and actions towards people based on fear instead of who they were. There were times I felt like I appeared desperate because I would bend over backwards to ensure the needs and wants of others were fulfilled, even if it went against what I felt was the right thing to do.

I would also do things just to avoid the feeling of not having control or like I didn't have a choice in the matter. This feeling of wanting to be in control stemmed from me being raped. I eventually realized that a person can only get away with what I allowed. I learned that I may not be able to control how people interact with me, but I could control my actions towards others. However, in order to do this, I would first have to change the way I thought. And that's exactly what I did.

I could have continued to internalize my bad experiences by blaming all my shortcomings on negative people, bad relationships, and life's challenges, but instead I chose to reflect on those things that caused so much frustration, hurt, and pain so that I could determine the lesson I should learn from those situations. The harsh reality is that I had always had the ability to live a life full of happiness, purpose, and love. In realizing this, I also realized that every hardship I endured was meant to build me, not break me.

My relationship with my father has never been a walk in the park. As a matter of fact, I spent years imagining what life would have been like if he had been present during all those pivotal father-daughter moments I craved to experience for the majority of my existence. Although I had male figures around me, no one ever filled the void my father created by not being present. *Let me clarify a bit.* I have always known of my father and even spent some moments with him. We even had a few in-depth conversations in which we were able to discuss some of our thoughts, experiences, and feelings. In the past, I didn't necessarily understand the value of our conversations, however, I have grown to realize that every interaction we had was valuable and necessary for my growth. In one of our interactions, my father made a statement that still sticks with me until this day. He said, "Actions speak louder than words."

I was in my early teens when he shared this with me. I knew what it meant, but I didn't truly grasp its meaning until later in life when instead of focusing on how negative I thought my father's actions were towards me, I decided to focus on what I believed his actions portrayed.

As I thought about all the times I desired for my father to be part of my life, I couldn't help but to wonder about what obstacles he struggled with daily. He, just like every other human being, is a product of his environment. Ultimately, I believe we were all created by God with His ordained purpose in mind. However, from a psychological perspective, our personalities are formulated from equations that consist of biology, our surrounding community, things we are taught, learned behaviors from everything we experience throughout our lives and how we process those things we experience throughout our life. If I could apply this concept to my life, why couldn't I view my father the same way? My father is a product of his environment and how he internalized his experiences. The only thing is, I have no idea what he had to face as a child leading into adulthood. However, one thing I do know is that he operated from a space that he felt was the right thing to do at the time.

When I began to look at things through this lens, it reduced my anger towards my father. This thing called life is not an easy journey for anyone.

It wasn't until I was able to see things from more than my perspective, that I was able to be content with everything that had transpired. Looking at things from more than one perspective tells me that everyone has more than one choice to choose from. There is a positive and negative way to operate in everything we do. Every action not only has a consequence, but it also has pros and cons when trying to figure out the best choice to follow through with.

Through my relationship with my father, I learned that a person's actions are a reflection of their heart, which is conditioned through life experiences that formulate thoughts. When a person exhibits negative actions towards someone else, it usually comes from a space of compiled thoughts based on their individual experiences. Many times, negative actions exhibited towards others have nothing to do with the person being violated. Instead, they are a true revelation and reflection of the individual exhibiting the negative behavior and how they see themselves. Realizing this helped me to understand that every action I take affects other people around me in some way. I have learned to utilize the notion that actions speak louder than words by connecting it with scripture.

**"Yes, just as you can identify a tree by its fruit,
so you can identify people by their actions."**
-Matthew 7:20

This scripture tells me that a person does what he or she thinks, and our thoughts are a reflection of our heart's desire. If our heart's desire is anything other than giving God the glory and dominion over everything about us by acknowledging Him in everything we do, then it will be extremely difficult to receive the blessing in store for us if we don't choose to follow His path.

This thought leads me to a time in my life when I felt like I was in complete bondage as a result of being violated in a way that caused much confusion and pain. During this period of my life, so many mixed emotions traveled through my mind because I couldn't understand how anyone could have their way with someone without their consent. This act of cruelty was not only played out by one person, but two guys. Now instead of focusing on the fact that I was raped, once again, I had to search for the lesson in the struggle. The years following that event made me feel worthless and as if the only thing men ever want is sex. This way of thinking spiraled into thoughts of feeling like I was worthless and unattractive.

Some may wonder how I could have felt unattractive when these men had imposed themselves upon me. The most common thought people may come up with is that they must have been physically attracted to me, but my thought process was different. I felt like I must not be attractive or likable because people don't treat things or people that way if they look at it as valuable or beautiful. A person who cherishes something treats it with care and nourishes it.

Let's look at this through the lens of love. By no means am I claiming that these two men loved me. However, I would like to take this time to discuss what love means and what it looks like. According to the Oxford Dictionary, love is *"an intense feeling of deep affection or a great interest and pleasure in something."* As a verb, it is to *"feel deep affection for someone."* Just by reading these definitions, it would lead a person to believe that an act of passion such as this suggests these men somehow loved me, and this was "supposedly" portrayed through their actions. However, my Bible tells me exactly what love looks like.

"Love is patient and kind.

Love is not jealous or boastful or proud or rude.

It does not demand it's own way.

It is not irritable and it keeps no record of being wronged.

It does not rejoice about injustice

but rejoices whenever the truth wins out.

Love never gives up, never loses faith, is always hopeful,

and endures through every circumstance."

-1 Corinthians 13:4-7

For me, love is much more than a feeling. Love requires certain actions to be exhibited in a person for it to be seen as love. However, there are different types of love, which means we are capable of loving others whether we know them or not.

To truly understand what love is, we must start with the love of God. The Bible gives numerous examples of what love looks like in different relationships. It also provides the ultimate example of love as exhibited through Jesus's sacrifice of laying down His life for every single one of us.

John 3:16 says, *"For this is how God loved the world. He gave his one and only Son so that everyone who believes in Him will not perish but have eternal life. God sent his Son into the World not to judge the world, but to save the world through Him."*

This helped me to refrain from being judgmental of other people's actions, and instead to learn from everyone's actions whether good or bad. I have my own choices and decisions to make. By no means am I saying that the behavior exhibited by these young men is right in any way. However, I did learn what love is through examples of people treating me with malice, hatred, jealousy, and judgement.

The Bible does an excellent job of giving us guidance on how to exhibit love through pure actions versus using the word love as just something to say or as a way to manipulate others.

I pointed out how God showed His love for us by sacrificing His only begotten son who died for our sins, yet I would like to take this love thing a bit further by explaining how I was able to come out of a mind space where I was afraid to trust myself. Instead of running away from attempting to build bonds or relationships with men, I had to learn to love myself first.

"You must love the Lord your God with all your heart, all your soul, and all your mind. This is the first and greatest commandment. A second is equally important: Love your neighbor as yourself."
-Matthew 22:37-39

I realized that I loved God and in loving God that consisted of me seeking God in everything, including how to love myself. Matthew 22:37-39 tells me to love my neighbor as myself. There used to be a time when I didn't grasp the meaning of this because I didn't even love myself. How can we have the ability to love someone else when most of us don't even know who we are as human beings?

Loving myself didn't happen overnight. It has been a lifelong journey. In learning how to love myself, I had to become more educated on who I am as a person. Referencing John 3:17 told me that Jesus was sent to this world not to condemn me, but to give me an example of how to love my neighbor. This scripture also provided a pure example of Jesus's worth. Jesus was a man who did not allow the opinions or actions of others to deter Him from fulfilling the purpose God sent Him on the earth to accomplish. Focusing on His purpose helped Him to remain focused and prevented Him from getting involved with things that had nothing to do with His purpose.

I discovered that making excuses for not following the will of God prevented me from fulfilling the purpose God predestined for me. I also realized that those excuses did nothing but prolong me from walking into the blessings God set out for me. It took me changing my thought process from carnal to a spiritually-minded way of thinking to see real transformation.

This means I had to stay rooted in the Word of God to avoid falling subject to society's standards. There are so many different statistics out here in this world, but I refuse to allow a statistic to dictate who I am. I am not a victim of my circumstances. Instead, I choose to be and operate as a child of the Most High God!

We hear people claiming to be a Christian, yet they pick and choose what commandments to follow based on convenience, self-pleasure, and greed. Even in this, God's Word does not change and remains the same. So, why do we try to make the Word of God fit us instead of being transformed by the Word of God? I know that if I was able to be transformed by the Word of God, then anyone else can do the same.

"For I was born a sinner, yes, from the moment my mother conceived me. But you desire honesty from the womb, teaching me wisdom even there."
-Psalms 51:5-6

This tells me that my natural desire is to sin, but God provides us with the wisdom to overcome sin.

In order to attain wisdom, we must remain open to hearing from God. The thing is, to consistently hear from God, requires us to acknowledge Him in all our ways and He will direct our paths.

"Trust in the LORD with all your heart and lean not on your own understanding; in all your ways acknowledge him, and he will make your paths straight."

-Proverbs 3:5-6

If we are not acknowledging God for direction, then we are following our desires, which without guidance from God, are often rooted in sin. I have believed in God for as long as I could understand who God is. The obstacles I have experienced over time have helped me to realize that miracles have always been a part of my life. My background has always included the backdrop of Christianity. I grew up in church to the point where it still feels weird if I am not in the church house on Sunday. I used to feel overwhelmed with how many church services I was forced to sit through, but as I matured, I grew to understand and appreciate the value of being in certain atmospheres to assist with the formation of my morals. My ability to understand what I read came naturally.

However, it took an intimate relationship with God and some challenges for me to truly understand scripture and its value.

This journey called life will always consist of ups and downs. Knowing this doesn't lessen the emotional impact of disappointments, conflicts, and rough times. The Word of God assisted me by guiding me through this path of divine purpose. Through the Word of God, I was able to learn to carry the Holy Spirit with me everywhere I go.

Let's focus a bit on this force called the Holy Spirit. I believe in the Trinity. God being the Father and the creator of all things sent His Son, Jesus, in physical form to earth with the purpose to die for our sins which transformed into life after death through the Holy Spirit. I can remember thinking as a child, how is reciting or learning scripture going to help me in the future? It wasn't until I was faced with challenges that I understood the meaning of scriptures like Philippians 4:13 which says, *"I can do all things through Christ who strengthens me."*

There was a season in my life when I had no choice but to rely on whoever God intentionally placed around me to assist with taking care of my home and child. In those moments, I can recall feeling helpless, discouraged, depressed, and broke. What I didn't know was all of this was part of God's divine order.

"Only I can tell you the future before it even happens. Everything I plan will come to pass, for I do whatever I wish."

-Isaiah 46:10

This scripture tells me that just as God purposefully blesses me, He can also purposefully allow me to go through some things to teach me and help me grow in areas of lack. As I understood the idea that everything happens for a reason, I began to question what exactly is the reason. Life has a way of constantly evolving whether we want it to or not. Although things are constantly changing, the truth is there is nothing new under the Son. I have learned my trials, tribulations, pain, and suffering are a direct result of God preparing me for things I have yet to experience.

I often say the only thing a person can control is themselves. This leads me to believe that everything around me is unpredictable. However, I can mold my own life. In molding my own life, Christianity is the basis on which I choose to formulate a direction to take based on what has and is taking place in my life. This just means the Bible, prayer and my relationship with God are what get me through every breathtaking moment of my life.

The Word of God has encouraged me throughout my life and is even more of a necessity to this very day. As growth continues to happen within my life, I become stronger in my ability to stand on the Word of God. My belief in God is unwavering because He is the only being who has not fallen short of His Word. Just because I believe in God, I read the Bible to get a better understanding of who He is and His expectations of me. As I have constantly sought God by studying His Word and praying, I have learned that everything I have experienced and will experience has always been divinely ordered.

2 Timothy 3:12-17 says, *"Yes, and everyone who wants to live a godly life in Christ Jesus will suffer persecution. But evil people and impostors will flourish. They will deceive others and will themselves be deceived. But you must remain faithful to the things you have been taught. You know they are true, for you know you can trust those who taught you. You have been taught the holy Scriptures from childhood, and they have given you the wisdom to receive the salvation that comes by trusting in Christ Jesus. All Scripture is inspired by God and is useful to teach us what is true and to make us realize what is wrong in our lives. It corrects us when we are wrong and teaches us to do what is right. God uses it to prepare and equip his people to do every good work."*

When this scripture was revealed to me, I couldn't do anything but praise the Almighty God. This scripture released a realm of comfort and relief; and truly helped me to turn all my negative experiences into positive ones.

This meant that nothing I went through was in vain. Every little thing I have experienced throughout my life has a purpose.

I'm going to harp on the *"actions speak louder than words,"* thing again. Although words hold a great deal of value, it is our actions that truly determine who or what we are loyal to. This is why I refuse to allow negative experiences to define or shape me in any way that causes me to be a statistic versus a conqueror. It's all about perspective.

The more I felt sorry for myself as a result of all the horrific things I had endured throughout my life, the more miserable I became. Nothing good ever came out of the toxic thoughts that invaded my mind. As I mentioned before, there was a period in my life when I felt useless and like I would be better off dead. And this was all because the things around me couldn't be controlled and I was operating under the pretense that if I gave people what I thought they wanted, then no one would ever take anything else from me again. This way of thinking still gave people and my past the right to have dominion over me because I gave it to them.

However, I learned to continuously fall back on the Word of God. My life experiences were there to build my character, so that it would align with God's purpose for my life. Those experiences were there, so I could learn to let my little light shine in good times and bad.